THE LITTLE GUIDE TO

elf

First published in 2024 by OH
An Imprint of HEADLINE PUBLISHING GROUP

2 4 6 8 10 9 7 5 3 1

Disclaimer:
All trademarks, copyright, quotations, company names, registered names,
products, characters, logos and catchphrases used or cited in this book are
the property of their respective owners. This book has not been licensed,
approved, sponsored, or endorsed by anyone involved in the creation, production
or distribution of Elf.

Elf is © Warner Bros. Entertainment Inc.

Cataloguing in Publication Data is available from the British Library

ISBN 978-1-03541-974-6

Compiled and written by: Malcolm Croft
Editorial: Saneaah Muhammad
Designed and typeset in Avenir by: Tony Seddon
Project manager: Russell Porter
Production: Rachel Burgess
Printed and bound in China

Headline's policy is to use papers that are natural,
renewable and recyclable products and made from
wood grown in well-managed forests and other
controlled sources. The logging and manufacturing
processes are expected to conform to the
environmental regulations of the country of origin.

HEADLINE PUBLISHING GROUP
An Hachette UK Company
Carmelite House, 50 Victoria Embankment, London EC4Y 0DZ

www.headline.co.uk   www.hachette.co.uk

THE LITTLE GUIDE TO

elf

the best of buddy

UNOFFICIAL AND UNAUTHORIZED

(OH)

CONTENTS

Introduction

Since its release in 2003, Jon Favreau's beloved *Elf* continues to grow in popularity with each new year and today sits high on its festive pedestal as the greatest Christmas comedy of the 21st-century. And for good reason, too. It's the very essence of the Christmas spirit distilled, crammed full of quotable one-liners bottled into a beautiful little bundle, a gift that keeps on giving well past its 97 minutes.

The star of this yuletide show is, of course, Buddy, widely considered to be everyone's favorite elf, who now represents Christmas better than anyone else. A human raised by elves at the North Pole, Buddy's story is the classic fish-out-of-water – a small-town hero's quest to redeem his naughty father in a wicked world far, far away (well, New York) while also trying to discover his inner (s)elf and help save his elderly, bearded mentor. OK, so it's basically the plot of *Star Wars*, but with Christmas spirit instead of the Force. Fine by us!

Welcome to *The Little Guide to Elf*, a compact celebration of everyone's favorite festive fairy tale in New York, a tiny tome crammed with so much syrupy festive cheer that you'll be sick in your Christmas stocking.

Stuffed with all the classic wit, quips, and wisecracks you love from Buddy and his friends, as well as a cast of real-world quotes and facts about the film's enduring legacy, this *Little Guide to Elf* is the perfect present for the *Elf*-mad member of your family, which, last time we looked, was everyone.

Happy Holidays and enjoy!

Chapter

1

Raised by Elves

While being cared for by nuns at an orphanage one fateful Christmas, infant Buddy's life changed forever when he climbed in Santa's sack to hold a teddy bear.

For 30 years, baby Buddy grew up, and up, *and up*, as he lived among the elves at the North Pole, believing himself to be one of them. All Buddy ever wanted was to feel normal, fit in, and find love, but when you're a human raised by elves, that's easier said than done.

This is Buddy's bonkers-but-brilliant backstory... and how it made him who he *really* is.

66

Oh, hello. You're probably here about the story. Elves love to tell stories. I'll bet you didn't know that about elves.

99

Papa Elf

narrating the first words spoken to the audience, and introducing the plot.

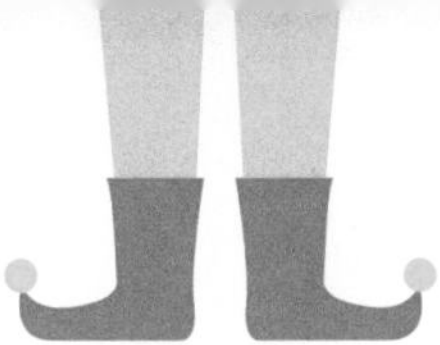

“We elves try to stick to the four main food groups: candy, candy canes, candy corns, and syrup.”

Buddy

to Emily, Walter, and Michael, over a plate of maple syrup spaghetti and a whole two-litre bottle of Coca-Cola. Will Ferrell felt very sick after shooting this scene multiple times.

Forced Perspective

Rather than employ CGI, director Jon Favreau used *forced perspective* to make Buddy appear bigger than the other elves, an optical illusion that manipulates human visual perception.

As Jon Favreau told *Rolling Stone* on December 24, 2020:
"You build two sets. One set is raised and closer and smaller, and one is bigger and further away. And if you line up those two sets and measure them, you can have one person on one set appear to be much larger than a person on the other set. We did that for all the shots at the North Pole."

"

You're not in the North Pole any longer. Look, you want to make me happy, don't you? Then lose the tights. As soon as possible.

"

Walter

to Buddy, requesting that Buddy get "rid of the elf costume". Buddy's reply: "But I've worn this my whole life." Buddy takes off his tights immediately and in front of Emily. Much to her horror.

"

Why not? He loves the snow. He's told me 15 times.

"

Walter

to Emily, in response to Emily's comment about Buddy: "Clearly he has some serious issues. We can't just throw him out in the snow."

> **"**
>
> Our goal, even then, was to make a movie that could be part of that pantheon. The fact that it's in rotation is the highest honor that movie can have.
>
> **"**

Jon Favreau
on the movie's everlasting legacy, interview with Gary
Susman, *Rolling Stone*, December 24, 2020.

Elf Humor #1

Who is Santa's favorite singer?

Elf-is Presley

"

When it comes to babies, Santa's a
pushover. So, Buddy stayed with an older
elf who had always wanted a child but had
been so committed to building toys, well, he
had forgotten to settle down. Yes, I raised
Buddy. I was his adopted father. Though
Buddy grew twice as fast, he wasn't any
different from the other children.

"

Papa Elf

narrating to the audience and telling them it is he,
Papa Elf, who raised Buddy when he was discovered in
Santa's sleigh that fateful Christmas Eve 30 years ago.

Elf on the Shelf

In 2005, the Lumistella Co released the "Elf on the Shelf" elf doll to accompany the self-published book written by Carol Aebersold and Chanda Bell and illustrated by Coë Steinwart. The book and elf toy were a global phenomenon, selling more than 30 million elf dolls.

The "Elf on the Shelf" story tells the tale of a "scout elf"* who reports to Santa which children have been naughty or nice, hence why now the elf dolls are placed in homes during the holiday season to keep an eye on children!

* The most popular name given to the "Elf on the Shelf" dolls is, of course, Buddy.

66

This place reminds me of Santa's workshop. Except it smells like mushrooms. And everyone looks like they wanna hurt me.

99

Buddy
dressed in a suit, is sent to the busy mailroom employees where everyone ignores him.
Though not for long.

Álfr

The oldest origin of the word "Elf" is believed to derive from Old Norse mythology, which told tall tales of short mythical creatures – *dǫkkalfar* (dark elves) and *ljósalfar* (light elves).

> I didn't know you had elves working here. Does Santa know that you left the workshop? Did you have to borrow a reindeer to get down here?

Buddy

to Miles Finch, a person of short stature, who Buddy believes to be an elf. An angry elf.

66

He's an angry elf... He must be a South Pole elf.

99

Buddy

to Walter, after Miles Finch storms out from Walter's important work meeting after Buddy repeatedly called him an elf. This was the last straw for Walter.

> It was less a challenge dressing Will due to his size and more a challenge to make sure nothing seemed off-putting or in bad taste. After all, I had to dress a grown man in tights and a cutaway coat. Needless to say, we did have a fair amount of fittings to be sure we struck the right balance between absurd and adorable.

Laura Jean Shannon
on dressing Will Ferrell for his role in *Elf*, interview with
Feel Christmassy, November 3, 2015.

Code of the Elves

1. Treat every day like Christmas.

2. There's room for everyone on the Nice list.

3. The best way to spread Christmas Cheer is singing loud for all to hear.

> **"**

There are only three jobs available to an elf. The first is making shoes at night while the old cobbler sleeps. You can bake cookies in a tree. As you can imagine, it's dangerous having an oven in an oak tree during the dry season.

> **"**

Papa Elf
narrating to the audience the jobs elves are capable of doing.

Elf Quiz #1

What has Papa Elf fitted to Santa's sleigh to help it fly?

1. SantaSpeed.

2. Kringle 3000.

3. Robot Rudolph.

4. Clausoboost 3000.

Answer: 2

❝

I put them on the
Naughty list, and they
never forgave me.

❞

Santa

about the Central Park Rangers, who chase Santa and
Buddy through the park as Santa's sleigh struggles to
get airborne. Thankfully, they take off just in time!

In the classic Christmas poem "A Visit from St Nicholas" (now popularly known as "'Twas the Night Before Christmas") written by Clement Clarke Moore in 1823, Santa is described as a "right jolly old elf".

This poem was the first to imply that Santa himself has elf-ish origins, a result of a possible merger with the Nordic folklore character Tomten, an elf-like spirit with a long white beard and a red hat that protected farming families and their animals thousands of years ago.

66

The third job [an elf can do], some call it 'the show' or 'the big dance'. It's the profession that every elf aspires to, and that is to build toys in Santa's workshop. It's a job only an elf can do. Our nimble fingers, natural cheer, and active minds are perfect for toy-building. They tried using gnomes and trolls. But the gnomes drank too much and the trolls weren't toilet trained.

99

Papa Elf
narrating to the audience the third job
elves are capable of doing – toy-making.

66

I'm getting too old for this job.

99

Santa

to Buddy, as he struggles to get his sleigh airborne
after the engine is gone. The line is an iconic one,
borrowed from the character of Roger Murtaugh
(Danny Glover) from the *Lethal Weapon* film franchise.

> **"**
>
> I remember running around New York in that outfit literally thinking, 'This is the end of my career.' In pointy shoes. In tights. I just knew it was a big roll of the dice. I loved this concept of a human raised at the North Pole who thinks he's an elf and finds out he isn't. But I had just come off of *Old School*, this R-rated crazy-man's film and now I'm doing this family Christmas movie. I knew it was either gonna really work or really fail.
>
> **"**

Will Ferrell
on filming *Elf*, interviewed by George Stroumboulopoulos,
George Stroumboulopoulos Tonight, CBC,
December 2013.

As seen in the orphanage at the beginning of the movie, Buddy takes his name from a brand of diapers – Little Buddy Diapers.

66

I don't care where you go. I don't care that you're an elf! I don't care that you're nuts! I don't care that you're my son! Get out of my life! Now!

99

Walter

angrily shouts at Buddy, after Buddy repeatedly called Miles Finch an elf and ruined Walter's important work meeting. Buddy runs away.

66

All right, all right. We've had
another very successful year.
So, after all that hard work, it's
time to start preparations...
for next Christmas!

99

Santa

to his elves in the North Pole workshop.
Santa allows elves a small break before getting
back to work for next year's Christmas.

Well, there's a rumor
floating around that that
the parents do it.

Papa Elf

to Buddy, answering his question "Who puts the
presents under the tree?" if humans no longer believe in
Santa. Buddy replies: "That's... that's ridiculous. Parents
couldn't do that all in one night. What about Santa's
cookies? I suppose parents eat them, too?"

66

Hey, Foom Foom? I hate
to do this to you, but you
think you could help me
pick up the slack on those
Etch A Sketches? Buddy
is killing me.

99

Ming Ming

to Foom Foom, talking about Buddy missing his
Etch A Sketch quota (he's 915 off the pace!). Buddy overhears
his friends talking about him and starts to doubt his elfishness.

"

Well, if he hasn't figured out he's a human by now, I don't think he ever will.

"

Foom Foom

to Ming Ming, about Buddy's true human identity, a fact that Buddy has yet to realize but has now overheard, causing him to faint onto his elf friend Pom Pom.

July 12, 1960

The day that Etch A Sketches were released in the U.S. The sketching toy features prominently and repeatedly in the movie.

Elves don't make the product in real life though. That honor belongs to Spin Master, a Canadian multinational children's toy and entertainment company.

Over 175 million Etch A Sketches have been sold to date.

66

Not now,
Arctic Puffin.

99

Buddy

to Arctic Puffin, who asks Buddy if he wants to pick some
berries. A running Buddy, of course, was too perturbed
by his newfound human-ness to play with his friend.
Jon Favreau voices the animated puffin.

39

66

When I read the script, I thought
Buddy had to be the most unjaded
creature. There's not a single cynical
part of him. I thought it must be
played in complete earnest, without
any winking to the audience in any
way. It had to be played straight.
And Jon Favreau shared the same
belief. Hopefully, the comedy would
come from his unjaded view of
things we take for granted.

99

Will Ferrell
on being Buddy, interview with Steve Head,
IGN, May 20, 2012.

40

66

Course you're not. You're
six-foot-three and had a
beard since you were 15.

99

Leon the Snowman

to Buddy, about the clearly visible human clues that
make it obvious to everyone but Buddy that he is not
an elf. Leon the Snowman is voiced by U.S. jazz
legend Leon Redbone.

"

At least you have a
daddy. I was just rolled
up one day and left out
here in the cold.

"

Leon the Snowman

to Buddy, complaining about his start in the life after
Buddy learns the identity of his human dad, Walter.

❝

Buddy, I've been around the
world many times when I was
a young cumulus nimbus cloud.
It's a wonderful place, filled with
wondrous creatures... except
dogs. Oh, by the way, don't eat the
yellow snow.

❞

Leon the Snowman

to Buddy, telling him that the learning of his true identity
could be the "golden opportunity to find out whom you
really are". Buddy agrees and his quest begins.

"

Oh, don't pay attention to Leon. He's never been anywhere. He doesn't have any feet.

"

Santa

to Buddy, after Buddy tells Santa that Leon described New York as "pretty different" to the North Pole. Santa of course has been to New York "a thousand times".

66

I told him his father had never
even known that Buddy was born,
and most importantly, I told him
where his father was - in a magical
land called New York City.

99

Papa Elf

narrating to the audience, and telling Buddy
(finally!) of his true origins and his human
backstory to kick the plot into action.

Fairy Tale in New York

Buddy's quest to find his naughty father, Walter, in New York is also a quest to discover his inner (s)elf.

While New York's Manhattan is considered the most Christmassy of places on Earth throughout December, it's also not, and Buddy's experience of the city that never sleeps is, well, anything but festive or family-friendly. No matter how hard he tries to fit in...

> **❝**
>
> Well, there you have it.
> Santa's in Manhattan.
>
> **❞**

Charlotte Dennon

the *New York One* reporter, on her first big news
story, telling news viewers that the object that fell
out of the sky was apparently Santa's sleigh.

66

So, I hear you're going on a little journey to the big city.

99

Santa

to Buddy, after he learns that Buddy is to leave
the North Pole and go on adventure to... New York!

66

I actually had to eat old
New York City gum. But it wasn't
as bad as you would think, still
relatively favorable. Good
to know if you ever have to eat
any gum off the streets.

99

Will Ferrell
on eating street gum, interviewed by Wilson Morales,
Blackfilm.com, November 2003.

❝

There are some things you should know about New York. First off, you see gum on the street, leave it there. It's not free candy. Second, there are, like, 30 Ray's Pizzas. They all claim to be the original, but the real one's on 11th.

❞

Santa

to Buddy, warning him to the dangers of New York City. In 2003, the famous Ray's Pizza, which opened in the 1970s, was located on Sixth Avenue and 11th Street, but it closed down in 2013. A Chinese restaurant occupies the space now.

$29 million

The sum that Will Ferrell turned down to return to the role of Buddy for an *Elf* sequel. Sorry, guys.

"I killed the idea of a sequel," Will told *The Guardian's* Jason Solomons (November 19, 2006). "$29m does seem a lot of money for a guy to wear tights, but it's what the marketplace will bear. I just think it would look slightly pathetic if I tried to squeeze back in the elf tights just to be Buddy, the middle-aged elf."

"

Hey, jack-weed, I get more action in a
week than you've had your entire life.
I've got houses in L.A., Paris, and Vail. Each
one of them with a 70-inch plasma screen.
So, I suggest you wipe that stupid smile
off your face before I come over there and
smack it off! You feeling strong, my friend?!
Call me elf one more time!

"

Miles Finch
angrily responding to Buddy's repeated belief
that Miles is an elf from the North Pole.

Gimbels, the department store where Jovie works in Santa Land, was the name of the store seen in (perhaps the ultimate Christmas classic) *Miracle on 34th Street*, released in 1947.

At the time, Gimbels, at 119 West 31st Street, was a rival to Macy's, the iconic New York department store a block north, but it closed down in 1987.

The name of the store was used in *Elf* as an homage to *Miracle on 34th Street*.

"

If you see a sign that says, 'Peep Show,' that doesn't mean that they're letting you look at presents before Christmas.

"

Santa

to Buddy, warning him to the exotic dangers around every corner in New York City.

"

Buddy is very forgiving and childlike and innocent, and that spreads to the whole city. And remember, that was a time when we were scouting, that was not long after 9/11. Having grown up in New York, it was so sad to me that people thought of Manhattan in how it related to 9/11. It was a city in mourning. And to go and make a movie about Christmas where the Empire State Building was something he dreamed about from a snow globe and his father worked there – it was almost like reclaiming Manhattan.

"

Jon Favreau
on the poignancy to the film's city setting, interview with
Gary Susman, *Rolling Stone*, December 24, 2020.

> **“**
>
> There seems to be a strange man dressed as an elf wandering through Central Park.
>
> **”**

News reporter

narrating footage of Buddy walking through Central Park looking for Santa's sleigh engine, in a manner identical to popular footage of Bigfoot being "captured" on camera. Jovie, watching at home, sees Buddy on TV and dashes out the door to Central Park.

Elf Humor #2

What type of music
do elves like best?

Wrap.

66

Listen, some people, they just lose sight of what's important in life. That doesn't mean they can't find their way again. Maybe all they need is just a little Christmas spirit.

99

Santa

to Buddy, informing him of human redemption, as well as foreshadowing the climax of the movie, and reminding the audience of the message of the movie.

Elf Quiz #2

What is wrong with the Kringle 3000's thermo-coupler at the start of the film?

1. It's long.

2. It's high.

3. It's got a short.

4. It's upside down.

Answer: 3

66

New Yorkers really care about Christmas. New York is way more Christmassy than L.A. L.A. is not cold, there's no gigantic Christmas tree, and no one is ice-skating. You have to drive to an indoor rink to go ice-skating.

99

Zooey Deschanel

on setting the movie in New York, interview with Rebecca Murray, LiveAbout, March 7, 2017.

"

You did it!
Congratulations!
'World's best cup
of coffee'. Great job,
everybody.

"

Buddy

to everyone at the coffee shop that displays a sign
reading "World's Best Cup of Coffee". The coffee shop
was actually located at 20 E Hastings Street in Vancouver,
Canada, where the scene was shot.

"

A song?
Anything for you, Dad.
I'm here with my dad,
And we never met,
And he wants me to sing him a song,
And, I was adopted,
But you didn't know I was born,
So, I'm here now, I found you, Daddy,
And, guess what? I love you!
I love you, I love you!

"

Buddy

to Walter, after he asks Buddy to sing a song as he
believes him to be a Christmas-gram when the two first
meet. The song was ad-libbed by Will Ferrell.

66

I think you're great, Charlotte. You're a great news lady. Yeah, your eyes tell the story. That's what I love about you. You've got a great mouth.

99

Matt Walsh

the famous TV actor before his big break, appearing as a cameo, flirting with news reporter Charlotte Dennon as he describes Santa's sleigh falling out of the sky.

66

What's a Christmas-
gram? I want one.

99

Buddy

to Walter, after hearing for the first time the words
"Christmas-gram". Buddy perhaps believes them to be
something more Christmassy than they actually are.

The cast and crew of *Elf* were not allowed to film inside, or use the name of Macy's, as the setting for the department store scenes in New York for one simple reason: the Fake Santa scene.

Macy's has to be seen as employing only the real Santa, otherwise kids would never go to see him. If the scene was cut, Macy's would have been used instead of the fictional Gimbels, but Jon Favreau deemed the scene too necessary.

66

Hey! Have you seen these toilets? They're ginormous!

99

Buddy

in a toilet cubicle at Gimbels, shouting at someone standing at a urinal.

> **"**
>
> Lynn Kessler wants a *Powerpuff Girls* playset. Mark Weber wants an electric guitar. Carolyn Reynolds wants a Suzy-Talks-A-Lot. Dirk Lawson wants a day of pampering at Burke Williams spa. Stan Tobias wants a power pumper water pistol.
>
> **"**

Michael

live on air to the whole of New York on the *New York One* news channel, reads out the Naughty and Nice list to prove Santa is real.

> ## Must be another Dirk Lawson.

Dirk Lawson

embarrassed and presumably drunk, while sat at a bar surrounded by other bar-dwellers after Michael reads out his name from Santa's Naughty and Nice list.

"

I like to whisper, too.

"

Buddy

to Walter and Walter's assistant Deb, moments before
Buddy is kicked out. An iconic line, perhaps because
of the way in which Will Ferrell really gets up close
into James Caan's face.

> 66

When we had Will [Ferrell] in the Lincoln Tunnel, the tunnel was open. Same thing with the 59th Street Bridge. Whenever he was out there in his suit, we'd hear screeches and fender-benders and lights smashing. People would be looking at him walking on the side and that would cause a few minor traffic accidents.

> 99

Jon Favreau
on Buddy's first arrival into New York and its
real-life reactions from city residents, interview with
Gary Susman, *Rolling Stone*, December 24, 2020.

66

I just like to smile, smiling's my favorite.

99

Buddy

to "Wanda" the Gimbels manager, when asked "Why you smiling like that?" The store manager wears the nametag saying "Wanda" because the original actor written for the role, Wanda Sykes, dropped out at the last minute. Fazion Love stepped into the role and played homage to Sykes with his nametag.

66

We had one take to destroy it. So, Favreau said, 'Just go nuts!'

99

Artie Lange
in an interview with *ABC News*, November 21, 2017.
It took the film's production team weeks to create and
decorate the Santa Land set in *Elf*, so when Buddy
realizes the store's Santa is a fake and a brawl starts,
it had to be filmed all in one take as they didn't
have time to fix or redecorate the set.

66

Make work your favorite. Work is your new favorite.

99

Wanda

Gimbels manager, to Buddy, in response to
Buddy's iconic line, "Smiling's my favorite."

66

Buddy, you're more of an elf than anyone I ever met, and the only one who I would want working on my sleigh tonight. Will you fix it for me, Buddy?

99

Santa

to Buddy, desperate for an elf's help to fix his sleigh so he can finish delivering presents. Buddy knows how, thanks to his Papa Elf.

> **"**
>
> I do play a jaded New Yorker. It's difficult to be in the Christmas spirit when your water's been shut off and you're being harassed by a gigantic elf. You have to take kind of a humiliating job to make ends meet.
>
> **"**

Zooey Deschanel
on her character Jovie, interview with Rebecca Murray,
LiveAbout, March 7, 2017.

66

By the way, I think you have the most beautiful singing voice in the whole wide world.

99

Buddy

to Jovie, in his most sincerest voice, after hearing Jovie sing "Baby, It's Cold Outside" in the Gimbels employee's bathroom.

44
per cent

The percentage of British people* who re-watch *Elf* every single year, according to an OnBuy study, 2020.

* Britons will spend around 14 days of their lifetime re-watching *Elf*.

66

Santa!!! Oh, my God!!!
Santa here?! I know him.
I know him.

99

Buddy

to the employees of Gimbels, upon hearing the
news that "Santa" is coming to town the next day.
The scene was completely improvised by Will Ferrell.
Sadly, Buddy's excitement is short-lived.

"

Get through? Christmas is the greatest day in the whole wide world!

"

Buddy

to Jovie, after Jovie mentions to Buddy that the holidays is just something to get through, not enjoyed. Jovie's response says it all: "Please stop talking to me."

"

I don't know if
I've played a character
that was constantly
eternally optimistic.
That actually was the
fun part of doing
the role.

"

Will Ferrell
on portraying the positivity of Buddy,
interviewed by Wilson Morales, Blackfilm.com,
November 2003.

"

I'm not messing with you. It's just nice to meet another human who shares my affinity for elf culture.

"

Buddy

to Jovie, upon their first meeting at Gimbels department store. Buddy's love for Christmas is not shared with his new co-worker... yet.

> **❝**
>
> Paul, don't tell him what you want. He's a liar. You disgust me. How can you live with yourself? You sit on a throne of lies. You're a fake. You stink. You smell like beef and cheese. You don't smell like Santa. He's an imposter! He's not Santa!
>
> **❞**

Buddy
to the fake Santa at Gimbels after he
realizes he's not the real Santa.

66

You sure it had nothing to do with the fact that I was naked in the shower?

99

Jovie

to Buddy, after Buddy tells Jovie that he went
to the bathroom only because he heard her singing
"Baby, It's Cold Outside".

66

It's pretty good. It's a
little too good. Corporate
must have sent in a
professional.

99

Wanda

Gimbels' manager, after spotting Buddy's flawless
work cleaning up the store's North Pole ahead
of "Santa's" visit.

"

Six-inch ribbon curls, honey.

"

Wanda

Gimbels manager, to Jovie, after noticing Jovie's gift-wrapping ribbon curls were under the expected length. A mirror to Buddy's low Etch A Sketch quota. Jovie's exasperated response: "That's impossible."

"

At the time, I was running around New York City in my yellow tights thinking, "This could be my last movie." Little did we know, we were making a movie that would stand the test of time, I think because it's beautifully uncynical. It's just very sweet and hopeful, and turns out it was funny.

"

Will Ferrell
on the legacy and success of *Elf* when it was released in 2003, *The One Show*, BBC, 2022.

66

No tomatoes. Too
vulnerable. Kids, they're
already vulnerable.

99

Miles Finch

to Walter, Eugene, and Morris, about the tomato idea
they pitched to Miles for a children's book.

> **"**
> What about this?
> A tribe of asparagus
> children, but they're self-
> conscious about the way
> their pee smells.
> **"**

Eugene Dupree

to Miles Finch, pitching Miles a book idea. A terrible,
terrible book idea. Eugene is played by comedian and
musician Kyle Gass, one half of comedy-rock band
Tenacious D with Jack Black.

Did you know?

Reindeers do not live in the North Pole.

The nearest possible location to the North Pole where reindeers do live is in Lapland, Finland, which is where many people who have drunk too much "Christmas spirit" believe Santa and his Christmas elves must originate from.

##

> Oh, fun? So felonies are fun now? I thought, see, felonies were felonies.

Walter

to Emily, after Walter learns that Buddy and Michael cut down a tree from the local park and brought it back to Walter's home to decorate as a Christmas tree. "At least Michael was happy for once," Emily says, attacking Walter.

$225 million

The box office tally of *Elf* when it was released in November 2003.

It quickly became the eighth biggest Christmas movie of all time and vastly returned on its original $33 million budget.

"

Look out, the yellow ones don't stop!

"

Buddy

to Jovie, about taxi cabs, as they run across
the street while on their date. Yellow is probably
not Buddy's favorite color.

Elf Quiz #3

The fearsome Central Park Rangers are said to still be under investigation after their controversial actions at which 1985 gig in Central Park?

1. Simon & Garfunkel.

2. The Rolling Stones.

3. Bruce Springsteen.

4. The Police.

Answer: 1

66

OK, picture this. We bring
in Miles Finch. The golden ghost.
We bring him in. He's written
more classics than Dr Seuss.
It ain't gonna be easy, but I think
it's worth a shot.

99

Walter

desperate, to his colleagues Eugene and Morris,
discussing the author Miles Finch, portrayed
with aplomb by Peter Dinklage.

95

"

The predominant one of New Yorkers was to walk right by me. If they didn't see a camera close by, people were afraid of me. They made a point of walking around me. I would walk up and hug people and they'd get really upset. A couple of times, they recognized me. People would look at me and say, 'Hey, aren't you that guy from *Saturday Night Live*? Have you gone completely insane?' There were some catcalls of, 'Nice tights.'

"

Will Ferrell
on the reactions of real New Yorkers to Buddy
walking through the streets of New York, interview with
Steve Head, IGN, May 20, 2012.

66

Hey, Bud, have you ever seen a mailroom? It's a place where mail from all over the world comes. And they sort it out there. And you can touch it all. And they put it in these shiny bins. I gotta work here. Maybe you can work... there.

99

Walter
to Buddy, after Walter has had enough of Buddy disrupting his working at his office.

Chapter

3

One Size Fits All

Elf may be consistently voted the No.1 Christmas movie of the 21st century so far, but it's the theme of family that really tugs at the heartstrings of this story. And Buddy's desire to find a one-size-fits-all family is all he wants this Christmas.

Wonderfully, by the end of the movie Buddy has two families – proof that, as the saying goes, "The family that laughs together stays together." And *Elf* has more family-friendly laughs than any other film...

66

Actually,
I'm adopted.

99

Buddy

to Walter and Santa, showing them both how much he's
grown thanks to his misadventures in New York and
finally come to understand and be proud of who he is.

"

I'll tell you what, why don't we just pull Michael out of school and let the deranged elf man raise him? Then they can have lots of fun committing felonies.

"

Walter

to Emily, discussing Michael's unhappiness at school and at home. Walter's answer only serves to further upset Emily.

"

I thought maybe we could make gingerbread houses, and eat cookie dough, and go ice skating, and... and maybe even hold hands.

"

Buddy

to Walter, after Buddy is bailed by Walter from jail for fighting with "Santa", much to Walter's horror.

❝

Can't wait to see my dad. We're gonna go ice skating and eat sugar plums.

❞

Buddy

to Santa, preparing to leave the North Pole and getting excited about the potential activities he'll enjoy once he meets his biological dad, Walter. Buddy is sure in for a surprise!

Elf Humor #3

What is Santa Claus' tax status?

Elf-employed.

"

That's the other thing
I wanted to talk to you
about. You know, Buddy,
your father... Well, he's on
the Naughty list.

"

Santa

to Buddy, giving him some bad news as he
prepares to leave the North Pole for New York.

"

It's me, your son. Susan Wells had me, and she didn't tell you. But now I'm here! It's me, Buddy.

"

Buddy

to Walter, upon their first meeting at Walter's work. Walter only remains interested in Buddy because he mentioned "Susan Wells", a former love of Walter's in the 1970s.

> ❝
> It's a boy...
> Buddy's your son.
> ❞

Dr Leonardo

to Walter, after confirming the results of the DNA test.
The proof Buddy needed, even if no DNA test on
Earth gets results that quick.

"

That's very impossible.
You saw that guy out
there. He's certifiably
insane.

"

Walter

to Dr Leonardo, after learning the conclusive
results that confirm Buddy is Walter's son.

66

Walter, just bring him home.
Introduce him to Emily and
Michael, and once he comes to
terms with reality, he should
drop the whole elf thing and
move on with his life.

99

Dr Leonardo

to Walter, in an attempt to reassure Walter
that Buddy's elfishness is not because
he is an actual elf.

Famous Elves

Buddy is perhaps the world's most famous elf, but he's not the only one...

1. Dobby, the House Elf
(Harry Potter, 2002)

2. Legolas Greenleaf
(The Lord of the Rings, 1937)

3. Link
(The Legend of Zelda, 1986)

4. Bernard, the Elf
(The Santa Clause, 1994)

5. Marcus Skidmore
(Bad Santa, 2003)

6. Hermey, the Misfit
(Rudolph the Red-Nosed Reindeer, 1964)

66

Oh, come on, Walter, I'm
sure he doesn't actually
think he's an elf.

99

Emily

to Walter, after being introduced to Buddy
for the first time at Walter and Emily's home.

"

As you know, we need a big launch fast to get the company back on track. So, I think I speak for my fellow board members when I say... this better be good.

"

Fulton Greenway

owner of Greenway Press and Walter's boss, to Walter, at the start of Walter's pitch. Just as Walter is about to start, Michael runs in and informs Walter that Buddy has run away. Walter then quits with a defiant "Up yours".

66

James Caan would
always give me a hard time
about it being called *Elf*.
'Why is it called *Elf*?'
I think he was embarrassed
about the title.

99

Jon Favreau
on James Caan's opinion of the film's
title, interview with Gary Susman, *Rolling Stone*,
December 24, 2020. (Not sure what else it could
have been called – it's about an elf!)

"

So where were
you for the last
30 years?

"

Emily
to Buddy, after watching Buddy guzzle an entire
two-litre bottle of Coca-Cola at the Hobbs' dining table.

"

I hadn't really
planned it out, but
I was thinking,
like... forever.

"

Buddy

to Emily, after she asks Buddy, "How long do
you think you'll be staying?" Buddy's answer
is not music to Walter's ears.

66

You never can tell, kid.
Tell me, Michael, what do
you want for Christmas?

99

Santa
to Michael, after he asks Santa if he's really real.

❝

So, Dad, I planned out our whole day. First, we'll make snow angels for two hours. And then we'll go ice skating, and then we'll eat a whole roll of Toll House cookie dough as fast as we can, and then, to finish, we'll snuggle.

❞

Buddy

to Walter, outlining his preferred activities for the day he hopes to spend with Walter from his Etch A Sketch list. Naturally, Walter has other plans.

In Scandinavian folklore, elves are considered to be magical house gnomes that protect homes from evil spirits. However, they are also cheeky pranksters with a love of pulling little tricks on humans, such as hiccups and bad dreams.

According to legend, if you leave a bowl of porridge in front of your door at night, the elves will leave you alone, and eat the porridge!

“

Well, he is on the Naughty list.

”

Buddy

to Michael, talking about Walter being the worst dad in the world. "All he cares about is money. He doesn't care about you, or me, or anybody," Michael tells Buddy.

"

My papa didn't make master tinker till he was 490.

"

Buddy

to his "best friend" in the mailroom, discussing their
rut-stuck careers after drinking way too much "syrup" in
his coffee, and having a tickle fight (for the first time).

How do you like them apples?

Santa

to Michael, after Santa shows Michael that he was on the Nice list and therefore deserves the present that he wrote Santa for – "a Real Huf board". Real is a brand of skateboard and Huf relates to pro-skater Keith Hufnagel, a friend of Jon Favreau's.

"

Buddy cares about everybody. All you care about is yourself.

"

Michael

to Walter, in front of Fulton Greenway, Walter's boss.
Walter must now decide what he loves more – his sons or
his job. We all know which way he goes.

66

Dad! I'm in love, I'm
in love, and I don't
care who knows it!

99

Buddy

to Walter, about Jovie, interrupting Walter's
important work meeting with Miles Finch.

> "
> When I heard that James Caan was going to be playing Walter I thought that was a stroke of genius. To have Sonny Corleone playing against this sweet, innocent elf? I had grown up watching *The Godfather*, and to think that James Caan was going to be in this movie was kind of insane to me. And, you know, it could not have worked better!
> "

David Berenbaum
Elf writer, on the casting of James Caan as Buddy's father Walter Hobbs, interview with *Radio Times*, December 23, 2022.

> Buddy, there's something I have to tell you right now. I didn't mean anything I said back there, not a word. I know you may be a little chemically imbalanced, but you've been right about a lot of things. I don't want you to leave. You're my son, and I love you.

Walter

to Buddy, after he and Michael find Santa's sleigh engine, and Buddy finds them. Much hugging, squeezing, and back-patting occurs.

12
seconds

The duration of the now-infamous Buddy burp after he guzzled an entire two-litre bottle of Coca-Cola. The burp was, in fact, burped by voice actor Maurice LaMarche, the voice behind Brain from the hit animated show *Pinky and the Brain*.

LaMarche is capable of such a sustained deep burp by creating a huge echo chamber inside his tongue and cheeks by twisting his tongue in such a way. He then creates a raspy sound at the back of his throat and bounces it around that echo chamber. Gross. But also hilarious.

66

And my firstborn,
he's an elf?

99

Walter

meeting Santa with Michael, double checks that his
first-born son is an elf. Santa confirms it to be true.

"

You know, he wasn't lying.

"

Walter

to Emily, about Buddy not lying about his elf
identity. Walter is relieved and Emily wishes
Walter a Merry Christmas.

❝

You missed.

❞

Jovie

to Buddy, after Buddy kisses Jovie – quickly on her cheek
– while ice skating at Rockefeller Center. Jovie then grabs
Buddy and gives him a proper kiss on the lips.

Right at the end of the movie, when Buddy is holding his baby daughter, we can see the infant is wearing a knitted hat with the word "Susie" on.

Buddy and Jovie named their first-born after Buddy's mum, Susan.

How sweet!

66

Officer Tom, this is my dad. This is
Walter... he came. He bailed me out.
They gave me one phone call. They gave
me one phone call, and I said, 'I know
who I'm gonna call... Walter Hobbs.' And
sure enough, you showed up. You did.
They said you weren't gonna show up.
They told me so many times...

99

Buddy

to Officer Tom and Walter, after Buddy is arrested
and sentenced for 24 hours as punishment for fighting
with "Santa" at Gimbels department store.

Chapter

4

Buddy Up

Buddy's growth from oversized elf to Santa's favorite little helper is a journey that takes as many twists and turns as putting up tangled Christmas lights around a tree.

From Buddy's beginnings at an orphanage to being raised by Papa Elf at the North Pole and then his quest to find his biological father and a family, Buddy's journey of (s)elf-discovery is as heartfelt as it is hilarious.

Let's chart it from the start...

❝

And then, I travelled through the seven levels of the Candy Cane Forest, past the Sea of Swirly-Twirly Gumdrops, and then, I walked through the Lincoln Tunnel.

❞

Buddy

to Emily, Walter, and Michael, at the dinner table at Walter's home. The line is echoed at the end of the movie when Buddy reads the "fictional" story of *Elf*, a book published by Walter about Buddy's journey from the North Pole to New York and "how he saved Christmas", to a classroom of children.

66

Can I listen to
your necklace?

99

Buddy

to Dr Leonardo, hilariously referring to the
doctor's stethoscope around his neck.

"

He's probably just
reverting to a state of
childlike dependency.

"

Dr Leonardo

to Walter, in an attempt to reassure Walter and explain
Buddy's elfish behavior.

66

Wow. You look miraculous.

99

Buddy

while dressed in a nice suit and hat, to Jovie, after greeting her outside her apartment for their Thursday date. He then takes her a cup of the "World's Best Cup of Coffee". Though it's actually a crappy cup of coffee.

In the hilarious scene
when Buddy is checking
the "Jack in the Box" toys
in Santa's Workshop,
director Jon Favreau used
a remote-control to trigger
the spring in the toys
to ensure the startled
reactions from
Will Ferrell were genuine.

66

I don't belong here.
I don't belong anywhere.

99

Buddy

to himself, feeling lonely as he stands on Queensboro
Bridge contemplating life, a scene identical to that
of George Bailey's in *It's a Wonderful Life*, and one
of many homages to that film. It's here that
Buddy sees Santa's sleigh crash in Central Park
and rushes to help him.

❝

I'm singing. I'm in a store, and I'm singing. I'm in a store, and I'm singing!

❞

Buddy

singing, rather out of tune and in several pitches, to a group of gathered children, in order to prove a point to Jovie about singing in public. Wanda, the Gimbels manager, runs over and shouts "Hey! There's no singing in the North Pole."

66

My finger has a heartbeat.

99

Buddy

to himself, after the doctor pricks Buddy's
finger to draw blood for a DNA test. The
result is shocking, if only for Walter.

David [Berenbaum], the writer, said he always had the movie *Big* in mind as something to emulate. He felt like I had some of those Tom Hanks qualities. When Jon Favreau and I first started talking, we agreed that if there was any movie we'd want to be compared to, it would be *Big* because that's such a nice film. It's funny but it works on a dramatic level as well.

Will Ferrell
on *Big*'s influence on *Elf*, interview with
Steve Head, IGN, May 20, 2012.

66

I knew you'd find it, Mr. Elf!

99

Santa

very happily, to Buddy, after Buddy delivers Santa's
crashed engine. Santa validates Buddy's identity as
an elf too, much to Buddy's happiness.

66

Great. I got a full 40 minutes. And I had time to build that rocking horse.

99

Buddy

to Emily, after Emily asks Buddy if he got any sleep.
As Emily speaks, Buddy serves Emily a bowl of spaghetti
with maple syrup. For breakfast. (And lunch.)

"

Buddy changing a lot of people in small ways and overall changing the personality of the city, that's something I think gives the movie heart.

"

Jon Favreau
on the film's central premise and how it gives the film an emotional resonance. Interview with Gary Susman, *Rolling Stone*, December 24, 2020.

66

Hey! What's your name? My name's Buddy. Oh! Does someone need a hug? Ah, ah! That's not cool! I just wanted a hug!

99

Buddy

to an aggressive raccoon he meets on his way to New York while walking through a forest. The noise the raccoon makes is actually that of a monkey.

“

It seems I'm not an elf.

”

Buddy

to Leon the Snowman, after Papa Elf tells Buddy
of his human-world origins and backstory.
News that Buddy does not take well.

66

No. But things worked out
pretty good. They gave
me a restraining order.

99

Buddy

to Jovie, after Jovie asks the forever-positive Buddy
"Did Gimbels give you your job back?" Buddy was kicked
out of Gimbels for fighting with "Santa" but
went back upon Michael's advice to see Jovie.

> 66
>
> I can't think of another actor who would be better playing the role than Will. Realistically, the movie doesn't work at all without Will Ferrell as Buddy the Elf. So to see him inhabit that role and really bring it to life was amazing. He just took it in unexpected directions and he has such an infectious energy that really just brought the entire thing to life.
>
> 99

David Berenbaum
on Will Ferrell's casting as Buddy, interview with
Radio Times, December 23, 2022.

Elf Quiz #4

When Buddy goes to Dr Leonardo's office for a DNA test, at Walter's request, Buddy eats cotton balls, much to Walter's anger. The cotton balls Buddy eats was actually just cotton candy that had not been dyed pink.

Question is: how many balls did he eat?*

1. Three.

2. Five.

3. One.

4. Six.

Answer: 1

"

I really wanted to see you.
I think you're beautiful.
I feel really warm when
I am around you, my
tongue swells up. So, do
you wanna go eat food?

"

Buddy

asking Jovie out on a date. Jovie blushes and
approves, but, rather weirdly, a time is not agreed
upon for their date on "Thursday". Buddy winks
when he says "food" because food is "code".

66

As much as Buddy was accepted by his family and friends, there were a few drawbacks to being a human in an elf's world.

99

Papa Elf

narrating to the audience, as an oversized Buddy works in a tiny workshop making Etch A Sketches. Forced perspective is used to show Buddy's larger-than-normal size.

66

I think it's time you start your tinker training. Santa's sleigh. You're gonna help me make it fly.

99

Papa Elf

to Buddy, enlisting his help to make Santa's sleigh fly, an important plot point the audience will need to remember at the end of the film.

66

No human being has ever set foot in Santa's workshop. That is until about 30 years ago, and, as you may have guessed, that's where our story begins...

99

Papa Elf

narrating to the audience, and introducing Buddy as an infant left at an orphanage with a gaggle of nuns. A nun calls Buddy a "Christmas Angel", which, as foreshadowing tends to go, he becomes at the end of the film when he saves Christmas.

66

Why don't you just say it?
I'm the worst toy-maker
in the world. I'm a cotton-
headed ninny-muggins.

99

Buddy

to Ming Ming, after falling 915 Etch A Sketches short of
the pace of his toy-making quota, just one of the several
drawbacks to being a "human in an elf's world".

> 66

I ingested a lot of sugar in this movie and I didn't get a lot of sleep. I constantly stayed up. But anything for the movie, I'm there. If it takes eating a lot of maple syrup, then I will if that's what the job calls for.

> 99

Will Ferrell
on his Buddy-esque diet while filming the movie, interviewed by Wilson Morales, Blackfilm.com, November 2003.

❝

So, good news! I saw a
dog today. Have you
seen a dog?

❞

Buddy

to Michael, after waiting for Michael for five
hours outside school in the hope of walking him
home and befriending him.

Buddy's Festive Playlist

Music plays an important part in *Elf*, so this holiday season, stick on Buddy's Festive Playlist, the second-highest-selling Christmas soundtrack album ever!

"Pennies from Heaven" – Louis Prima

"Sleigh Ride" – Ella Fitzgerald and the Frank De Vol Orchestra

"Let It Snow! Let It Snow! Let It Snow!" – Lena Horne

"Sleigh Ride/Santa Claus' Party" – Ferrante & Teicher/Les Baxter

"Baby, It's Cold Outside" – Leon Redbone and Zooey Deschanel

"Jingle Bells" – Jim Reeves

"The Nutcracker Suite" – Brian Setzer Orchestra

"Christmas Island" – Leon Redbone

"Santa Baby" – Eartha Kitt and the Henri René Orchestra

"Winter Wonderland" – Ray Charles

"Santa Claus Is Comin' to Town" – Eddy Arnold

"Nothing from Nothing" – Billy Preston

And how could we forget...

"Whoomp! There It Is" – Tag Team

Elf Humor #4

What is the first thing elves learn in school?

The elf-abet.

66

Ow! Son of a
nutcracker!

99

Buddy
in pain, after being hit in the face by a snowball
thrown by Michael's school bullies. An iconic line,
if absolutely meaningless.

66

Buddy the elf, what's your favorite color?

99

Buddy

scrambling across Walter's desk at his office to pick up his work phone. They hang up. And Buddy is sent – dun dun duh! – to the mailroom.

66

I'm sorry I ruined your lives and crammed 11 cookies into the VCR. I don't belong here. I don't belong anywhere. I'll never forget you. Love, Buddy.

99

Buddy

writing an Etch A Sketch a message for Walter, Emily, and Michael, after Walter shouted at Buddy to leave and get out of his life.

When the original script for *Elf* was first written in 1993, ten years before the film was released, script-writer David Berenbaum had Canadian comedian Jim Carrey in mind to be Buddy. Carrey became the biggest actor in the world with *Ace Ventura, Dumb and Dumber,* and *The Mask* in 1994 – all in the same year!

❝

I'm not an elf, Santa.
I can't do anything right.

❞

Buddy

to Santa, no longer believing in himself as an elf
or a human, after running away from the Hobbs family
for "ruining their lives" (and cramming 11 cookies
into the VCR).

Chapter

5

Spirited
Away

What is Christmas without a Christmas
spirit? It's a load of old humbug that's what!
Thankfully, *Elf* is stocked full of the
Christmas spirit.

From Buddy and Michael's unshakeable
belief, to Walter's redemption, to Jovie
(quite literally) finding her voice and Santa's
sleigh being physically lifted by it, the
Christmas spirit is the fundamental force
that fuels the film.

So, let's get into the Christmas spirit this
holiday season, and dive right into it...

66

And so, with a little help, Buddy managed
to save Christmas. And his spirit saved
a lot of other people, too. Walter started
his own independent publishing company.
His first book was written by a brand new,
critically-acclaimed children's author.
The book was *Elf*, a fictional story about
an adopted elf named Buddy who was
raised in the North Pole, went to New York,
ate spaghetti, worked in a shiny mailroom,
and eventually saved Christmas.

99

Papa Elf

narrating to the viewer, perfectly summing up the events of
the film, while Walter and Jovie sing "Auld Lang Syne".

66

You have such a pretty
face. You should be on
a Christmas Card.

99

Buddy
to Walter's assistant, Deb. He just can't help
spreading Christmas cheer.

66

Christmas spirit is about believing, not seeing. If the whole world saw me, all would be lost. The paparazzi have been trying to nail me for years.

99

Santa

to Michael, discussing the real meaning of Christmas: Christmas is for life, not just the holidays.

66

Boy, am I glad to see you, Buddy. The Claus-o-meter suddenly just dropped down to zero. There's just no Christmas spirit anymore. And then the strain was too much, the engine broke free of her mounts. I need an elf's help.

99

Santa

to Buddy, after crashing his sleigh in Central Park, an event Buddy thankfully saw while standing high up on Queensboro Bridge.

66

Before the turbine days, this baby used to run solely on Christmas spirit. You believed in me. You made my sleigh fly.

99

Santa

to Michael, moments before Michael runs off
with the Naughty and Nice list. Total naughty move.

66

Well, silly as it sounds, a lot of people down south don't believe in Santa Claus.

99

Papa Elf

to Buddy, implying that 21st century humans in the real world have all become a little cynical and jaded when it comes to believing in Santa Clause, and therefore there isn't as much Christmas spirit as there once was.

66

You're not singing. You're just moving your lips!

99

Michael

to Walter, after he catches Walter not singing with Jovie, and therefore not helping the Christmas spirit lift Santa's sleigh. In the next cut, Walter sings merrily.

" It's important for the economy. Yes. "

Will Ferrell
when asked "Do you think it's important that children believe in Santa?", interviewed by Wilson Morales, Blackfilm.com, November 2003.

66

Just like the old days!

99

Santa

to Buddy, just as his sleigh zooms off into the night above the streets of New York, airborne with the Christmas spirit thanks to Jovie and the crowd's singing. Santa is, of course, referring to the good old days when the sleigh was held aloft by pure belief in Santa alone.

> "
> Hopefully we have made a movie that people are going to find funny and something that can be a shared experience for the entire family in a way that's emotionally satisfying as a story but also works as a comedy and captures the spirit of the holidays, all kind of rolled into one.
> "

Will Ferrell
on his pre-release hopes for the film's success,
interviewed by Wilson Morales, Blackfilm.com,
November 2003.

177

66

I thought the magical
reindeer made the
sleigh fly?

99

Buddy

to Papa Elf, double-checking the audience understands
a key plot point: that while magical reindeer help make
Santa's sleigh fly, they require the Christmas spirit of
humans to become magical. Got it?

> **“**
> If you sing alone,
> you can sing in front
> of other people. There's
> no difference.
> **”**

Buddy

to Jovie, as Jovie attempts to get Buddy out
of her way. As we all know, come the end of
the film it is Jovie's singing that causes the
Christmas spirit to help Santa's sleigh fly.

“

Someone mentioned
to me that I didn't blink
for the entire film, which
I wasn't conscious of,
but that's just something
that manifests itself in
whatever way it's going to
once I'm in character.

"

Will Ferrell
on Buddy's quite literal wide-eyed view of the world,
interviewed by Wilson Morales, Blackfilm.com,
November 2003.

180

66

If you're really Santa Claus,
then we can just get some news
cameras in here, and everyone
will believe in you, then your
sleigh will fly, right?

99

Michael

to Santa, discussing Santa's crashed sleigh. Moments
later, Michael runs away with the Naughty and Nice
list to share it with the world.

66

It's him, it's the real Santa!
His sleigh won't fly, 'cause nobody
believes in him! Everyone out
there, Santa needs us to believe,
I can prove he's real. Look,
this is his list!

99

Michael

to *New York One* reporter Charlotte Dennon, and live
on air to the whole of New York. Michael reads out the
Naughty and Nice list to prove Santa is real but without
him being caught on camera.

66

Buddy, he's in the park
with Santa. The sleigh
won't fly 'cause there's no
Christmas spirit.

99

Michael
to Jovie, after they meet in Central Park. Jovie
starts to sing "Santa Claus is Coming to Town",
thereby overcoming her fears of singing in public.

183

＂

Wow. That's a big one.

＂

Buddy

to Jovie, on their date, after skipping all the way to
Rockefeller Center to see the large Christmas tree
and go ice skating… and have their first kiss.

> **"**
>
> I was really missing East Coast winters. I was not used to L.A. winters at all. I sort of missed the family and everything like that and so I essentially surrounded myself with all sorts of Christmas movies. And then I started writing one.
>
> **"**

David Berenbaum
on the reason he wrote the first draft of *Elf*
in the early 1990s, interview with *Radio Times*,
December 23, 2022.

185

Elf Humor #5

What goes inside
elves' pointy shoes?

Their mistletoes.

Due to the enduring success of
the movie, in 2010, *Elf: The Musical*
made its debut on New York's
Broadway to much critical and
commercial applause.

It ran for two years on Broadway,
and then in London's West End during
2015-2016. Versions of it still tour
the world today.

In the musical, Buddy's infectious
Christmas spirit is given a name
- Sparklejollytwinklejingley!

Fayophobia –

a fear
of elves.

> **66**

Every year less and less people believe in Santa Claus. We have a real energy crisis on our hands. I mean, just see how low the Claus-o-meter is. That's why I came up with this little beauty in the 60s. It's a Kringle 3000. A 500-reindeer power jet turbine engine. Without it, the sleigh couldn't get more than a few feet off the ground.

> **99**

Papa Elf

to Buddy, about the volume of Christmas spirit becoming so low Papa Elf has had to invent a powerful engine that powers Santa's sleigh instead of regular spirited fuel. Don't try to think about it too much, it's a bit of a plot hole.

66

Oddly enough,
I hate Christmas.
That's the irony
of all this.

99

Will Ferrell
on his love of Christmas,
interview with Steve Head, IGN,
May 20, 2012.

66

Sounds like someone needs to sing a Christmas carol... The best way to spread Christmas cheer is singing loud for all to hear.

99

Buddy

to Jovie, as Jovie appears unconvinced by the healing power of the Christmas holiday. "Thanks, but I don't sing," she responds, lying.

"

Oh, it's not a costume.
I'm an elf.
Well, technically,
I'm a human, but I was
raised by elves.

"

Buddy

to Carolyn, a little girl he meets
in Dr Leonardo's office for a DNA test
at Walter's request.
Carolyn's response: "I'm a human
raised by humans."

192